D1180794

Purple Ronnie's
Little Guide for

Lovers

♡

First published 1999 by Boxtree
an imprint of Macmillan Publishers Ltd
25 Eccleston Place London SW1W 9NF
Basingstoke and Oxford

www.macmillan.co.uk

Associated companies throughout the world

ISBN 0 7522 17291

9 8 7 6 5 4

A CIP catalogue record for this book is
available from the British Library

Text by Giles Andreae
Illustrations by Janet Cronin
Printed and bound in Hong Kong

Being Fancied

If you want people to fancy you – it is best to be as mysterious as possible

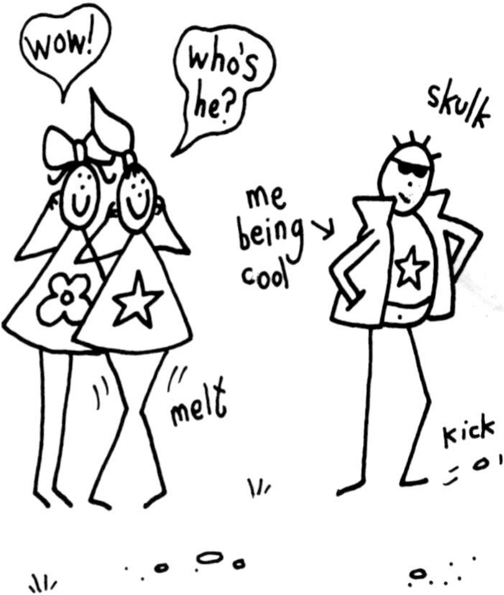
wow!
who's he?
skulk
me being cool
melt
kick

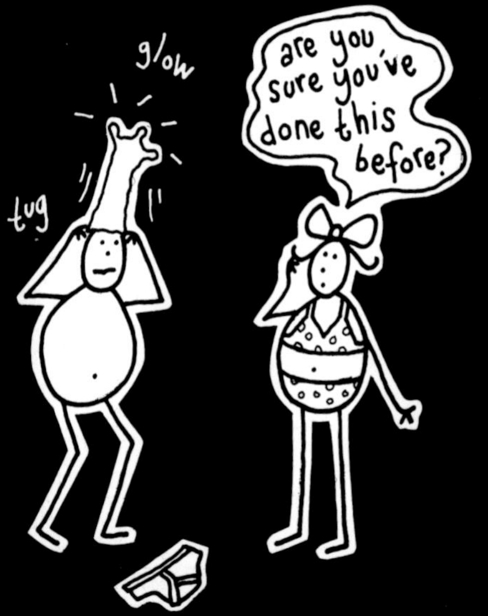
glow
tug
are you sure you've done this before?

a poem about

Safe Sex

To make sure you're safe
when you DO IT
Put on a Thingie that fits
I like the ones that can
glow in the dark
With the slippery nobbly
bits

Girls Beware:-

Most men need a lesson in how to make you feel special

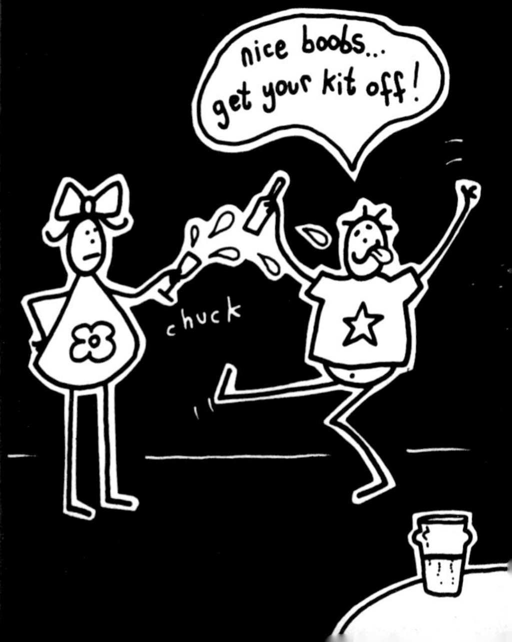
nice boobs...
get your kit off!
chuck

a poem about
SĚX

Some people are just hopeless
When you get them in the
sack
They'd always rather
watch T.V.
Or have a boring chat

Men Beware :-

Girls always have sneaky ways of catching the men they fancy

you're so cool and handsome and funny and clever and tough and manly etc etc etc
smitten

a poem about

Loving You

How many ways do I love you?

I think there are probably
two

The rumpety-pump way

Is all very well

But I like the soppy way
too

<u>Important</u> :-

Try not to dribble too
much when you are
snogging...

a poem about
Snogging

It's funny how us people

Show our love by touching
tongues

But at least we're not all
doggies

Or we'd sniff each others'
__bums!__

Remember :-

Everyone has secret places where they like to be touched...

a poem about
Love ↓ Handles

Some people think they're
not sexy
Unless they're as skinny
as candles
But I think it feels
much nicer

To cuddle some squidgey
Love Handles

Special Tip for Men

Girls like their lovers to be romantic and exciting...

...It is not _always_ best
to be incredibly skilful

a poem to say

I Love You

Sometimes when it's late
at night
And we're alone together

I want to take you in
my arms
And cuddle you forever ♡

Positions

You can Do It in all sorts of different positions

... some are more
complicated than others

a poem for
My Lover

The smashing thing about you

That makes me think
you're great

Is you're not only my
lover

You're also my best mate

Love Tip

Remember that nobody
likes being taken for
granted...

... give your lover lots of treats and surprises

a poem about
Kissing

Some kisses last for just
seconds
They're gentle and go on the
cheeks
But I like the ones you put
right on the lips
That can go on for 2 or 3
weeks

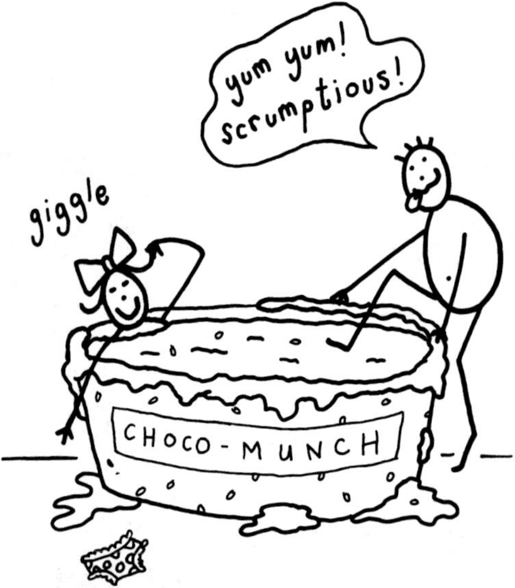
yum yum! scrumptious!
giggle
CHOCO-MUNCH

a poem for ↓

My Scrumptious Lover

You're so unbelievably gorgeous

I thought that I'd just have
to say

I'd love to submerge you
in chocolate

And lick it off slowly
all day

Special Tip for Men

Try not to fart and fall asleep straight after Doing It...

...most girls do not like that

a not too soppy poem to say

I Love You

This poem says I love you

And you make my life
complete

Except for all your
bottom burps

And your stinky feet

Special Tip for Girls

If you tell a man he is
brilliant in bed...

...he will do anything
for you

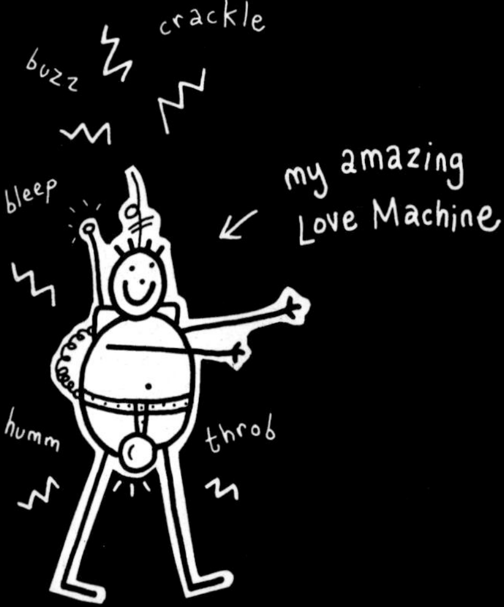
crackle
buzz
bleep
my amazing
Love Machine
humm
throb

a poem for a
Lover

If someone invented a
gadget

That made me terrific in
bed

I think I'd buy twenty-five
thousand

And Do It with you till
I'm dead